MW01283986

Brimming with creative inspiration, how-to projects, and useful information to enrich your everyday life, quarto.com is a favorite destination for those pursuing their interests and passions.

First published in 2022 by Wide Eyed Editions, an imprint of The Quarto Group.
100 Cummings Center, Suite 265D, Beverly, MA 01915, USA.
T +1 978-282-9590 F +1 078-283-2742 **www.Quarto.com**

ISBN 978-0-7112-6984-2

Illustrated with colored inks
Set in Budidaya and Slopes

Published by Georgia Amson-Bradshaw
Designed by Belinda Webster
Edited by Alex Hithersay and Lucy Brownridge
Production by Dawn Cameron

Manufactured in Guangdong, China TT062022

1 3 5 7 9 8 6 4 2

CLAIRE COCK-STARKEY
ILLUSTRATED BY SAMANTHA DOLAN

WIDE EYED EDITIONS

CONTENTS

FORESTS

SEAS AND OCEANS

MOUNTAINS

HILLS AND VALLEYS

RIVERS AND LAKES

WETLANDS

BETUSHKA AND THE WOOD MAIDEN

a Czech tale

In a tiny ramshackle hut next to the woods lived Betushka and her mother. Every day Betushka would take her goats into the forest to graze while she spun flax into thread on her spindle. Betushka had very little money but she was a happy soul. As she walked through the woods she would revel in the beauty of nature, singing and dancing all the while.

One day she noticed a beautiful grove of birch trees. She sat down under the swaying branches and began to work. After a while, she looked up to check on her goats, and her gaze was met by a lovely maiden with long flowing hair and a crown of flowers atop her head.

"I see you singing and dancing every day and it makes me smile," she said warmly. "Won't you put down your spindle and dance with me?"

Betushka took the lady's hands and followed her into the birch grove. The birds in the trees gathered and sang for them as they whirled and twirled together all day, never needing to stop for a rest.

The lady appeared again the next day and held out her hands for Betushka to join her in a dance, but Betushka shook her head sadly. "I cannot dance today for I must catch up with my spinning." The maiden told Betushka not to worry and the birds started to sing. Betushka couldn't resist the melody, and together they danced.

As the sun went down, they finally stopped and Betushka was full of happiness–until she remembered her empty spindle. Seeing her sadness, the maiden took the wooden spindle and by some magic, the flax was transformed into a spool of perfectly spun thread. "Oh, thank you!" Betushka cried, and she skipped home.

The following morning the lady was at the grove waiting for her, and the pair spent another glorious day dancing among the trees. At the end of the day, the lady again filled the spindle with thread. "How can I ever thank you?" Betushka asked.

"It is I who must thank you for dancing so joyfully with me," the lady replied. "I have put something in your basket to show my gratitude. Now go home to your mother."

When Betushka returned home and her mother saw her glowing cheeks, she asked her what had happened. Her mother's eyes widened as Betushka told the tale. "What luck: you have danced with the Wood Maiden!" she cried. Betushka showed her the spindle of fine thread and as they unspooled it they realized it would never run out. Next they lifted the lid of the basket, and inside they found a pile of birch leaves turned to gold. Betushka and her mother cried with happiness, for they knew that they would never go hungry again. Betushka's mother hugged her daughter tight, proud in the knowledge that only those with the purest hearts get to dance with the Wood Maiden.

CREATION STORIES OF FORESTS

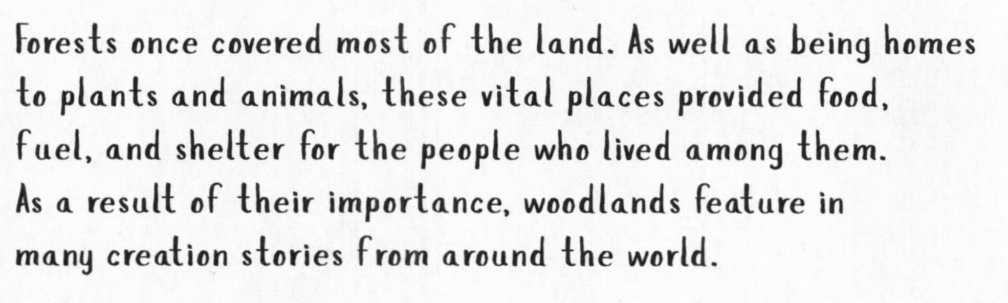

Forests once covered most of the land. As well as being homes to plants and animals, these vital places provided food, fuel, and shelter for the people who lived among them. As a result of their importance, woodlands feature in many creation stories from around the world.

In Lithuanian folklore, Medeina is the "mother of the forests." She looks after all the trees, plants, and animals that reside in the woods, protecting them from hunters.

In Norse mythology, Yggdrasil is the enormous ash tree that holds the whole cosmos together. Its snow-tipped canopy rises above the clouds, and its roots burrow into the depths of the underworld.

Cernunnos is the Celtic God of the Forest. He has long shaggy hair and beard and wears a crown of antlers. He embodies the forest and acts as guardian to all the animals within it.

A tale from the Patawomeck people of Virginia tells that humans were created by the Great Hare. Until the forests were ready, he kept the people in a sack. The Great Hare made a deer but his fellow gods hunted and killed it. He sprinkled the deer's hair throughout the forest and from each strand sprang a new deer. Then, he let the humans out of the sack to live in harmony with the deer in the forest.

In Māori tradition, the goddess Papatūānuku (earth) and god Ranginui (sky) had such a tight embrace that they squashed their children in the darkness between them. Tāne and his siblings decided to push their parents apart, letting in the light and allowing life to flourish. To hold up the sky, Tāne created all the trees and so he is god of the forests.

Mayan legend tells that when the forests were first created, they were too quiet, so the gods filled them with animals. When the gods asked them to say their names, the animals only growled, barked, and chirped. Annoyed, the gods created humans who could speak and worship their creators.

WOODLAND FLOWERS

During spring, beautiful woodland flowers emerge, enticed out by sunshine hitting the forest floor before the trees have fully come into leaf.

The flowers of wood anemones close up at night and during rain storms. English folklore says that fairies climb into the flowers and close them up to shelter from the rain.

When it is time for the fairies to gather in the woods, the bluebell tolls. But beware! If a human follows the sound of the ringing bells into the forest, they will never be seen again.

In England, foxes were thought to wear foxgloves on their feet to protect their paws from dew and allow them to silently sneak up on their prey.

In Irish tradition, the speckled marks on the foxglove flower were said to be the tiny handprints left by fairies.

Red campion only grows in the oldest forests and is an indicator of ancient woodland. It was said that red campion planted around a beehive would act as protection for the bees' honey stores.

In Bohemia, ferns were believed to flower on Midsummer's Eve. If you picked the golden fern flower and climbed a mountain with it clutched in your hand, you would be certain to discover treasure.

In German folklore, primroses are known as the "key flower" because of their ability to open fairy doorways and reveal hidden treasures.

Native to the forests of North America, *Erythronium albidum* is known as white fawn lily or white trout lily because its large mottled leaves look like the markings seen on fawns and trout.

FUNGI, LICHEN, AND MOSS

The damp, dark depths of woodlands encourage the growth of fungi, lichen, and moss. The interesting look and texture of these ancient organisms have inspired many folktales to explain their origin.

In England, it was said that fairies danced within circles of fungi, each toadstool acting as a seat on which the tired fairies could stop and rest for a while.

Japanese folklore says that if lightning hits the forest floor, it will make the mushrooms multiply.

Mushrooms have a habit of growing in circles. In Austrian tradition, these formations are known as witches' rings, in France they are sorcerer's rings, and in English folklore they are called fairy rings.

In Indigenous American Tejas legend, North Wind was an old man with long hair. He came south every winter, bringing cold air and laying down his blanket of snow. One spring, warm South Wind decided North Wind had stayed too long, so he took a deep breath and blew him away. North Wind's long hair fell off into the forest, forming clumps of Spanish moss.

Lung wort is a leafy lichen with lung-shaped leaves. Indigenous Canadian Gitxsan people call it "frog's dress" or "frog's blanket." In Europe, it is a sign that the forest is ancient.

Usnea is another type of lichen which grows on trees and looks like hair. It has many folk names, such as old man's beard, seaweed of the mountains, and witches' whiskers.

Sphagnum moss grows in Irish peat bogs and has long been known to have antiseptic properties. Right up until World War I, it was collected and used as a bandage to heal wounds.

WOODLAND SPIRITS

Perhaps because of the rustling of the leaves and the swaying of the trees, forests have long been thought to harbor all sorts of spirits. However, not all of them have friendly intentions.

Dryads are forest nymphs in Greek mythology. Each dryad is bound in spirit to one tree from which they rarely stray. Their bond is so strong that if the tree dies, so does its dryad.

Tapio is a Finnish forest spirit who has lichen for a beard and moss as eyebrows. Tapio is the protector of all woodland animals.

The Enchanted Forest of Arthurian legend is said to be full of bewitching fairy maidens. Any knight who is enticed to follow a fairy will be doomed to wander forever, lost amongst the trees.

In Brazilian Tupi mythology, Anhangá is a forest spirit who appears as a white stag with red eyes. It was said that Anhangá would punish anyone foolish enough to hunt animals with young by sending them mad.

Tengu are Japanese spirits who live in mountain forests. They have long noses, and often red faces and large wings. They love to cause chaos by waving their huge fan to stir up wild and dangerous winds.

In Danish lore, elves are known as huldre and dwell in the forest. They look beautiful from the front, but from the back they appear as hollow as a lightning-blasted tree trunk.

Baba Yaga is a witch from Slavic folklore who lives deep in the forest in a hut that stands on magical chicken legs and is surrounded by a fence made from bones.

MYTHICAL WOODLAND CREATURES

Not only are our woods and forests said to be teeming with enchanted spirits, but they are also thought to provide a home for a wide variety of magical creatures.

Forest-dwelling satyrs have a human body, horse's ears, and two horse's legs. In Greek mythology, satyrs are companions of Dionysus, the god of wine and celebration. Therefore they can often be found dancing, feasting, and making merry.

The curupira is a forest guardian from Brazilian mythology who preys on hunters who try to take too much from the forest. He has bright orange hair and his feet are back-to-front, so anyone trying to follow his footprints will walk the wrong way, allowing him to stay safely hidden.

The forests of Germany are home to the wise Moss Folk. They are hard to spot in their tree homes because their faces are covered in moss, their hair and beard are lichen, and their limbs resemble the branches of trees.

In Cajun folklore, a "loup-garou" werewolf stalks the forest. This werewolf doesn't depend on the full moon but can shapeshift at any time. If a hunter spills the blood of a loup-garou, they will turn into one for 101 days.

In Greek mythology, centaurs are half-human, half-horse. Chiron was one of few wise and good centaurs and he shared his wisdom with heroes such as Achilles and Heracles. During a battle, Heracles accidentally shot Chiron with an arrow. The god Zeus released him from the endless pain caused by the poison and set him in the sky as the constellation Sagittarius.

WHY THE SEA MOANS

a Brazilian folktale

On a beautiful island surrounded by crystal clear waters lived a lonely princess named Dionysia. Every day she would sit on the beach wishing for a companion and imagining that the gently lapping waves were saying her name: "Di-o-ny-si-a." Aching with loneliness, she cried out to the sea for a friend.

To her surprise, the waves parted and an enormous sea serpent slithered onto the shore. Dionysia was not afraid–after all, she had asked for a friend. Every day the serpent, Labismena, came and spent the whole day playing with Dionysia, and they became the best of friends.

On Dionysia's sixteenth birthday, Labismena said they were now too old to play but she promised Dionysia that if she ever needed her, she just had to come down to the beach and call her name. With tears in her eyes, Dionysia waved goodbye to her dear friend.

Some years later an old king came and asked Dionysia to marry him. She did not want to marry the old king, but her father insisted.

That night she sneaked down to the shore and whispered, "Labismena," to the waves. Her old friend appeared and advised her to tell the king she would not marry him until he found her three dresses–one the color of the fields and all the flowers, one the color of the sea and all the fish, and the last the color of the sky and all the stars. It took the king months to find such rare dresses, but he did and he came to claim his bride. Once again Dionysia stole down to the sea and called, "Labismena." This time, Labismena produced a small boat and told Dionysia that if she sailed across the sea she would land on an island and there she would meet her true love.

"How can I ever thank you?" Dionysia cried, as tears of gratitude coursed down her cheeks.

"There is one thing you could do for me," Labismena replied. "I am not really a sea serpent at all but a princess like you. I am under an enchantment that can only be broken when the happiest girl in all the world says my name three times. The day you find true love you will be the happiest girl in the world; if you say my name, I will be free."

Dionysia promised Labismena it would be so, hugged her tightly, and set off in the little boat. Just as Labismena predicted, Dionysia fell in love. But in her happiness Dionysia forgot her old friend and never said her name again.

To this day, Labismena lives as a sea serpent in the ocean. Every now and then she remembers how her friend forgot her and she groans. When you are next near the ocean, listen carefully and you might hear the waves whisper, "Di-o-ny-si-a," as they lap upon the beach, together with the sad moan of Labismena, remembering her betrayal.

CREATION STORIES OF SEAS AND OCEANS

Many creation stories begin with a world entirely covered in vast, swirling oceans. This represents the chaos at the beginning of time. When the land is formed, harmony is brought to the universe.

In Indigenous American Haudenosaunee tradition, it was said that the whole world was once covered in water. Only Muskrat could dive deep enough to touch the bottom. Turtle volunteered to let Muskrat pile earth on top of him and Turtle grew bigger and bigger until, finally, all of North America was formed.

In Hindu mythology, the creator Vishnu lives in a corner of the never-ending sky. Using his thoughts alone he created a cloud, and where the shadow of this cloud fell he made a great ocean. This ocean was not like an ordinary ocean. Instead, it was full of the waters of creation from which Vishnu could fashion every living thing.

In Egyptian mythology, when the world began there was nothing but endless, churning water. This water was the first god, Nun, whose name means "primeval waters." Nun represented disorder, but from his waters emerged Re, the Sun god. Re brought order to the world by creating land and all life on Earth.

Celtic mythology tells that before any living thing existed there was sea and there was land. When the sea met the land, a white horse formed from the sea foam. This white horse became the first living thing to emerge onto Earth.

SEAWEED, SHELLS, AND CORAL

The products of the sea conjure up powerful sensory reactions: seaweed emits a strong salty smell, and shells, when held to the ear, recreate the sound of the waves. As a result, seaweed, shells, and coral have been highly prized for their seemingly magical powers.

Hawaiian mythology tells of a woman who gave birth to a shark. She wrapped it in seaweed and released it into the water, where it wore the seaweed like a green coat. From that day on, the shark acted as an aumakua, or guardian spirit, to the woman's family—as long as they never again ate shark or seaweed.

In Ireland, there is a tradition of hanging seaweed or kelp on a nail outside the door to predict the weather. If the seaweed becomes wet and flexible, rain is on its way.

An Aztec legend tells that Quetzalcóatl needed bones to create modern humans. Lord of the Underworld, Mictlantecuhtli, refused to give him any bones unless he could make a sound from a conch shell. Quetzalcóatl summoned worms to make holes in the shell and bees to buzz inside it. You can still hear the sound of the bees if you hold your ear to a conch shell.

Between the eighth and twentieth centuries, cowrie shells were a currency in parts of West Africa. Hunters also wore the shells as a protective charm and fortune-tellers predicted the future by reading the shapes made by scattered shells.

In ancient Greece, red coral was believed to be magical because it had formed from the blood of the snake-haired Gorgon, Medusa, which seeped into the sea after Perseus cut off her head.

In the past, some sailors would wrap a piece of coral in seal skin and tie it to the ship's mast. This was thought to protect the ship from storms, strong winds, and tempests.

SEA GODS AND GODDESSES

The wild and unpredictable nature of the sea is reflected in the gods and goddesses said to rule over the oceans in world mythology.

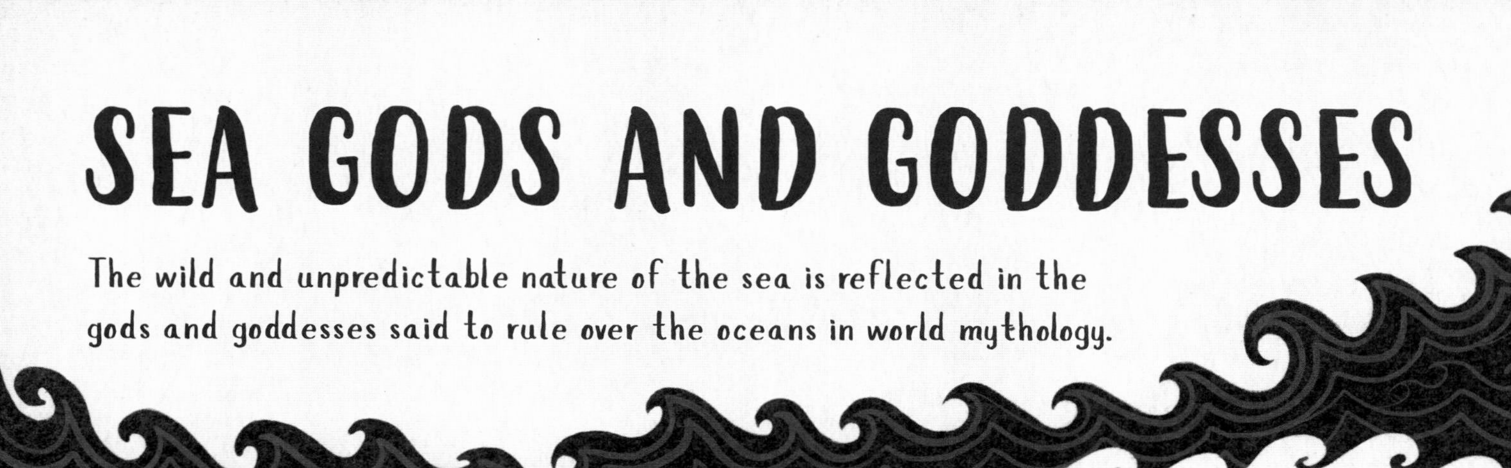

Ægir and his wife Rán were Norse sea gods who lived in a wondrous underwater palace. Ægir was generous and kind, while Rán was sinister, using her magical net to capture and drown sailors. Their nine daughters, the Billow Maidens, controlled the waves.

Manannán mac Lir was a sea god and king of the Otherworld in Irish mythology, whose name means "son of the sea." He sailed a self-propelled boat called Wave-sweeper and owned a cloak of invisibility.

Ryūjin is a Japanese sea god and dragon king. He resides deep in the ocean and controls the tides using a large jewel. Snakes act as Ryūjin's messengers, bringing him news from the land.

In Māori legend, Tangaroa is a sea god who fathered all the fish and all the reptiles. When his reptile children fled to the forests and were sheltered by his brother Tāne, god of the woodlands, Tangaroa was furious. He takes great pleasure in sinking canoes made from the wood from Tāne's forests.

Greek goddess of the sea Amphitrite married Poseidon after he sent a dolphin to fetch her. She is often depicted driving her husband around in their magical chariot, pulled by seahorses.

MERMAIDS

Folklore from around the world is full of mermaid-like creatures. Some say this is because people caught glimpses of seals or dugongs and were mistaken, but others will swear that mermaids are real.

Most European mermaids are half-woman, half-fish. They live underwater but occasionally sit on rocks to sing and comb their long hair. Some sailors say seeing a mermaid during a voyage foretells bad luck or shipwreck.

Ceasg is a Scottish mermaid with the upper body of a human but the tail of a salmon. To protect herself from harm she keeps her soul safely concealed in an object hidden under the sea. Anyone who finds the soul of a ceasg can make her grant them three wishes.

Merrow are Irish sea fairies with fishy tails and lurid green hair. These mermaids and mermen possess a magical cap that allows them to live underwater.

Selkies are similar to mermaids and come from the Orkney Islands. They swim in the ocean in seal form, but can cast off their seal-skin to dance on the beach in the shape of humans.

In Māori tradition, marakihau are guardians of the sea with fish-like tails and human upper bodies. They suck up huge quantities of fish with their long hollow tongues, much to the annoyance of local fishermen.

Japanese mermaids are known as ningyo. They have the body of a fish with the face of a monkey. It is considered extremely unlucky for a fisherman to catch a ningyo.

MYTHICAL SEA MONSTERS

Sailors exploring the vast oceans often returned with tales of enormous sea serpents and other watery horrors. These fantastical creatures were thought to reflect the many dangers posed by the wild seas.

Scylla was one of the most feared sea monsters in Greek mythology. She attacked passing ships with her six heads on the end of long, snake-like necks. Scylla was once a nymph but she was transformed into a monstrous sea creature by the jealous sorceress Circe.

In Norse mythology, Jörmungandr was a poisonous sea serpent who grew to encircle Midgard (Earth). It was foretold that when he stops holding his own tail in his mouth and comes to land, Ragnarök–the end of the world–will begin.

Leviathan is a gigantic sea serpent from Jewish tradition. It was covered in thick scales, had huge glowing eyes, and could breathe fire, causing the waters around it to boil.

The kraken is a legendary Norse sea monster in the form of a giant octopus. It was so huge that hapless sailors would mistake it for an island. Anyone stepping foot on the kraken would be pulled underwater by its tentacles.
Sailors in Japanese folklore fear the lurking umibozu (sea monk) who rises suddenly out of calm seas and upends boats. Umibozu can reach 30 feet in height, and they loom out of the water like an enormous black shadow with two glowing white eyes.
A dendan is a sea monster from Arabian legend who lurks in the depths of the ocean. It is said that the gigantic dendan can swallow an entire ship and her crew in just one mouthful.
In Chinese legend, shen is a shapeshifting dragon who transforms into a giant clam and causes mirages with its breath.

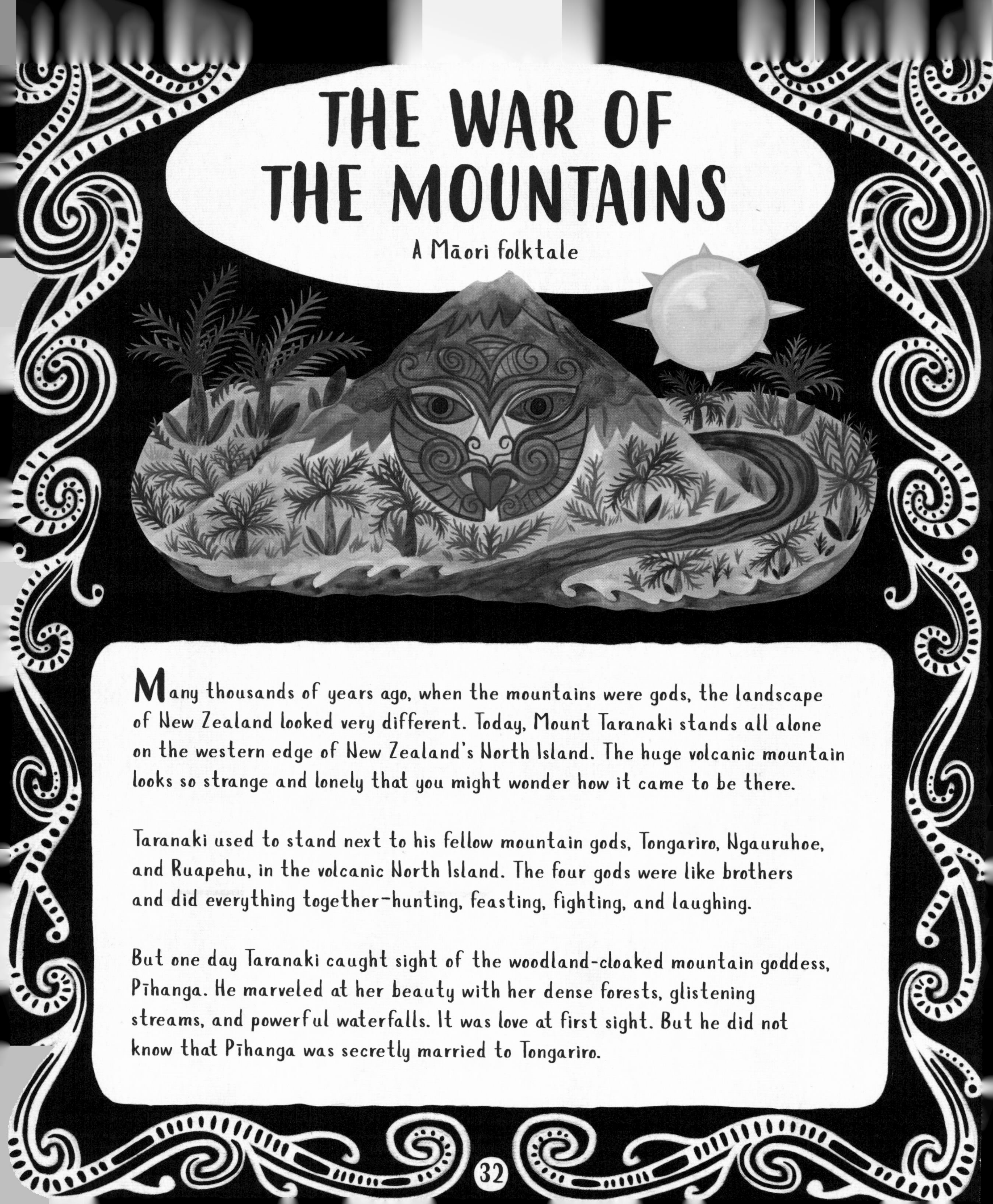

THE WAR OF THE MOUNTAINS

A Māori folktale

Many thousands of years ago, when the mountains were gods, the landscape of New Zealand looked very different. Today, Mount Taranaki stands all alone on the western edge of New Zealand's North Island. The huge volcanic mountain looks so strange and lonely that you might wonder how it came to be there.

Taranaki used to stand next to his fellow mountain gods, Tongariro, Ngauruhoe, and Ruapehu, in the volcanic North Island. The four gods were like brothers and did everything together—hunting, feasting, fighting, and laughing.

But one day Taranaki caught sight of the woodland-cloaked mountain goddess, Pīhanga. He marveled at her beauty with her dense forests, glistening streams, and powerful waterfalls. It was love at first sight. But he did not know that Pīhanga was secretly married to Tongariro.

Sick with love, Taranaki wove stories of the blissful future he and Pīhanga could have together. Tongariro overheard Taranaki's stories and was furious. How dare Taranaki try to steal his beautiful wife from under his nose! The fire and brimstone deep within him flared up and spilled over, scorching the land all around him as he bellowed, "Stay away from my wife!"

Taranaki was shocked that his beloved Pīhanga was married and felt he must fight for her. A battle broke out between the gods which raged for many days and nights. Finally, Taranaki was defeated.

With a bruised heart, Taranaki began to move away across the North Island. He dragged his heavy, battle-scarred body through the landscape, carving out a deep gorge as he went. His bitter tears flowed endlessly, filling the channel and creating the great Whanganui River.

At last, he came to a small peninsula near the sea. Here he settled down to rest and as he slept the ground grew around him and rooted him to the spot. And there he stays, many miles from his former friends, all alone.

Still he yearns for Pīhanga, wishing one day that he might return to her side. For that reason many Māori communities avoid living around the base of Mount Taranaki, just in case he one day decides to heave up his great rocky body and drag it back to his former home, destroying everything in his path.

CREATION STORIES OF MOUNTAINS

The dramatic shapes and impressive size of the world's mountain ranges have inspired some wondrous stories to explain how they were formed.

In a Swiss folktale, the clumsy giant Cervin crashed through a huge pile of earth. All that was left was a mountain between his legs: the unusually triangular Matterhorn, or Mont Cervin.

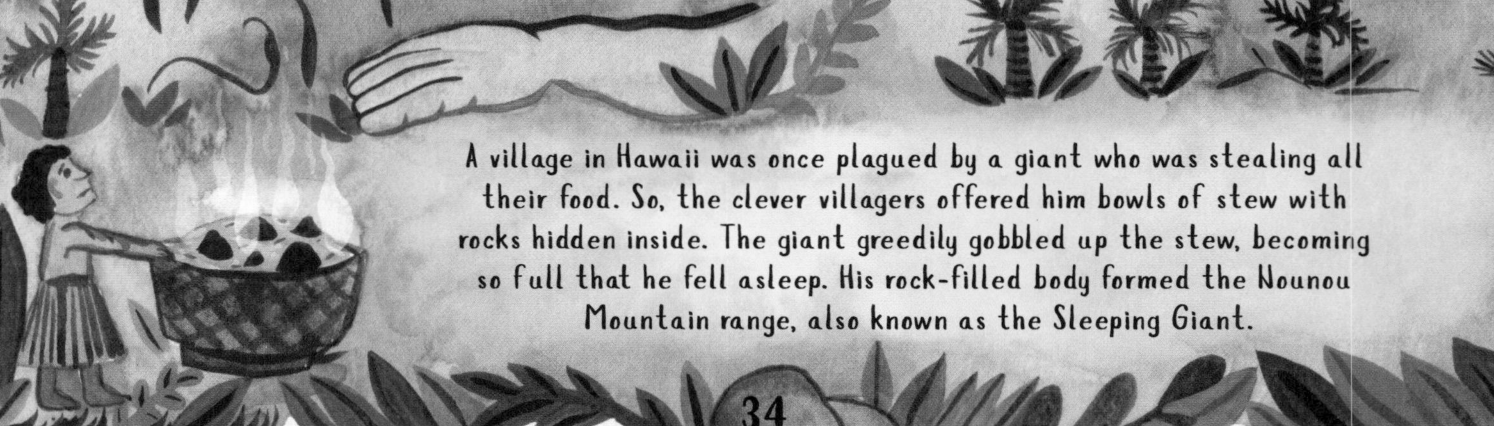

A village in Hawaii was once plagued by a giant who was stealing all their food. So, the clever villagers offered him bowls of stew with rocks hidden inside. The giant greedily gobbled up the stew, becoming so full that he fell asleep. His rock-filled body formed the Nounou Mountain range, also known as the Sleeping Giant.

In Chinese mythology, Pangu was the first man to exist. He hatched out of an egg and then pushed apart Heaven and Earth, placing the sun, the moon, and the stars in the sky. Next, he used his hands to dig out the valleys and build huge mountains, shaping the landscape.

Cherokee legend tells that when the Earth was covered by a flood, a great buzzard flew down to collect some earth to make land for the animals. As the bird swooped down his wings were sucked into the mud, creating valleys. When he flew off, the dried mud from his wings fell to the Earth and became mountains.

In a South African Xhosa tale, the creator god Qamata placed a giant at each corner of the globe to protect his creation. Cape Town's famous Table Mountain is said to be the body of the largest giant, known as Umlindi Wemingizimu, which means "Watcher of the South."

SACRED MOUNTAINS

Towering majestically into the sky, mountains are often believed to be the homes of the gods, bridging the gap between Heaven and Earth.

Mount Olympus, the highest mountain in Greece, was the home of the gods in Greek mythology. Olympus is a magical place where the Olympians live in marble palaces, feast on ambrosia, drink nectar, and because they are feisty gods, quarrel!

In Greek mythology, the Hippocrene was a spring on Mount Helicon, formed when the winged horse Pegasus struck the mountain with his hoof. It was sacred to the Muses–goddesses of the arts, science, and literature–and anyone who drank its waters would receive poetic inspiration.

Mount Sinai is one of the holiest mountains in Islam, Christianity, and Judaism, as it is where Moses was said to have received the Ten Commandments from God. Although Mount Sinai is described in many holy books, its true location remains a mystery.

In the Shinto religion of Japan, the kami (spirit) of Mount Fuji is the beautiful Konohanasakuya-hime. Some people make offerings to her at her shrines on the sacred mountain, believing she will prevent it from erupting.
In Hindu, Buddhist, and Jain tradition, Mount Kailash in the Himalayas is believed to be the cosmic axis where Heaven and Earth meet. Gods and holy people are thought to live at the very top of the mountain. Buddhists believe that Mount Kailash has the power to absorb a lifetime's worth of sin.
In Norse tradition, the mythological Niðafjöll (dark mountains) are found in the underworld. There lives the dragon Níðhöggr who gnaws at the base of the world tree, Yggdrasil.

GIANTS, TROLLS, AND DWARVES

The rocks littering the sides of mountains are often taken as evidence of argumentative trolls, dwarves, and giants who are said to live there, angrily tossing boulders at one another.

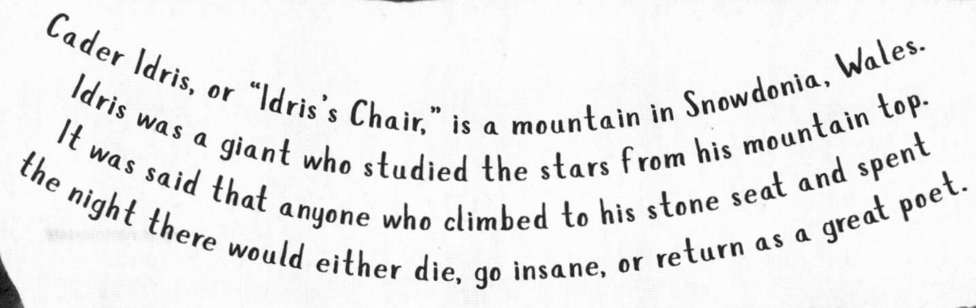

Cader Idris, or "Idris's Chair," is a mountain in Snowdonia, Wales. Idris was a giant who studied the stars from his mountain top. It was said that anyone who climbed to his stone seat and spent the night there would either die, go insane, or return as a great poet.

Chenoo are stone giants of Haudenosaunee legend. They live in the mountains and cause them to echo and rumble as they fight amongst themselves. Chenoo hate to be seen by humans, so if one comes near they will freeze and blend in with the rocky landscape.

The svartálfar (dark elves) from Norse mythology were born from the maggots that ate the flesh of the dead giant Ymir. The gods banished them to live in caves under the mountains.

Scandinavian folklore tells that slow-witted trolls live in remote mountains. Although strong enough to use trees as clubs, trolls are afraid of lightning, the ringing of church bells, and above all, sunlight, which turns them to stone. Many of the craggy boulders found on mountainsides are said to be trolls who were caught outside after sunrise.

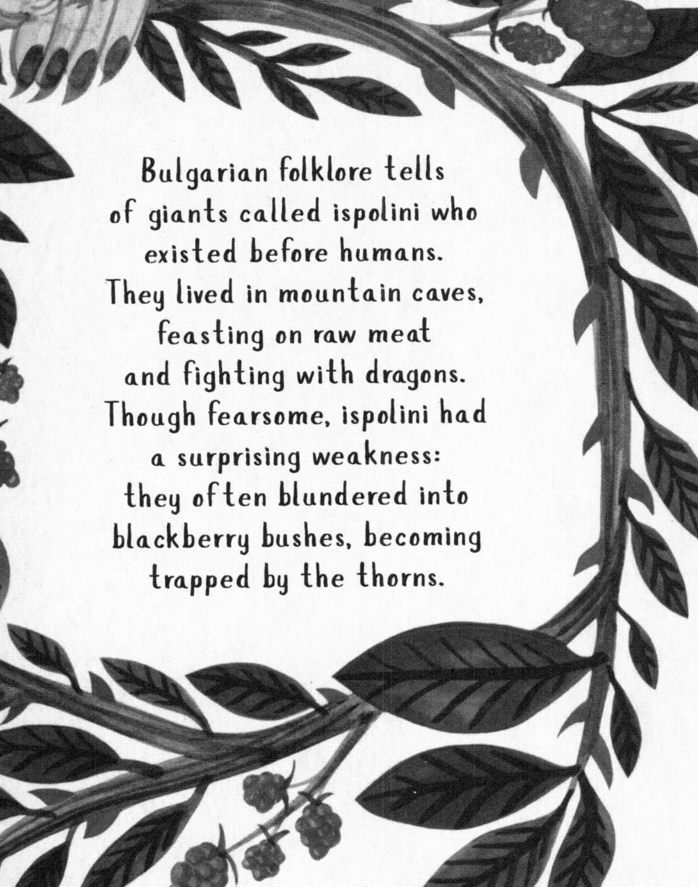

Bulgarian folklore tells of giants called ispolini who existed before humans. They lived in mountain caves, feasting on raw meat and fighting with dragons. Though fearsome, ispolini had a surprising weakness: they often blundered into blackberry bushes, becoming trapped by the thorns.

In Germanic lore, dwarves dwell deep under mountains in marvelous palaces. Here they make magical weapons and armor.

VOLCANOES

The dramatic sight of a volcano erupting, spewing out ash, smoke, and red-hot lava, has inspired many myths and legends of the creatures, gods, or goddesses who might dwell within.

Pele is the Hawaiian goddess of volcanoes. When Pele is angry she causes eruptions and stamps her feet to cause earthquakes.

She is both a creative and destructive force because her burning lava ravages the Earth, but as it cools it becomes solid and makes new land.

Māori legend tells of Kuiwai and Haungaroa, two sisters whose brother, the medicine man Ngātoro, tried to climb a mountain. When the cold nearly killed him, the sisters sent fire demons through the ground to spew from the mountain and warm Ngātoro, forming the volcano Ngauruhoe.

Hephaestus was the Greek god of volcanoes and blacksmiths. He made many wondrous weapons in his forge beneath Mount Etna, including Hermes' winged helmet, Achilles' armor, and Eros's bow and arrow.

The Aztecs believed that two volcanoes, Iztaccíhuatl (the White Lady) and Popocatépetl (the Smoking Mountain), used to be a princess and a warrior who fell in love. When they died, the gods turned them into mountains. Popocatépetl releases plumes of smoke to show that he still watches over his love, Iztaccíhuatl.

The Itelmen of Russia believed that demons known as gomuls live on top of volcanoes. Each night, the demons fly down to catch whales and fish, which they cook over the fires from their volcanoes.

It is said that the Indonesian volcano Mount Bromo was created by an ogre who was madly in love with a princess. She told the ogre she would marry him if he could dig a crater in the mountain top in one night. When the ogre nearly achieved the task, she made the cockerel crow early, signaling that day had come.

MOUNTAIN SPIRITS

World folklore tells of many different spirits who lurk in the mountains. Some are kind and helpful, but others are to be feared.

Rübezahl is a shapeshifting mountain spirit of Germanic origin. He brings sunshine or storms depending on his mood. To keep him happy, you must call him "Lord of the Mountains"—and never "Rübezahl" which means "turnip counter!"

In Norse mythology, Skadi is a winter goddess who lives in the highest reaches of the mountains, where the snow never melts. Silently roaming the slopes in her snowshoes, Skadi often leads stranded climbers to safety.

Barbegazi are mountain spirits who live in the French-Swiss Alps. They wear white fur clothes for camouflage, and long icicles hang from their hair and beards. Barbegazi use their large feet as skis, and often warn humans of avalanches or rescue lost climbers.

In German folklore, Bergmönch ("mountain monk") is an enormous spirit whose flaming eyes peer out from beneath a monk's hood. His breath is poisonous, and he has long been feared by workers in the mines where he dwells.

Achachilas are the protective spirits of the Aymara people from Bolivia. From beneath the Andes mountains, they control the coming of rain, frost, and hail. Achachilas sometimes take the shape of old men, or appear in dreams to warn of danger.

In Hindu mythology, an airi is the ghost of a hunter who roams the mountains with his ferocious pack of ghost hounds. Most mortals who cross an airi's path die of fright–but those brave enough to survive the shock may be rewarded, as he might lead them to his cave full of treasure.

Yama-uba is a Japanese mountain spirit with snakes for hair. Her serpents are said to seize lost travelers and pull them into her mouth.

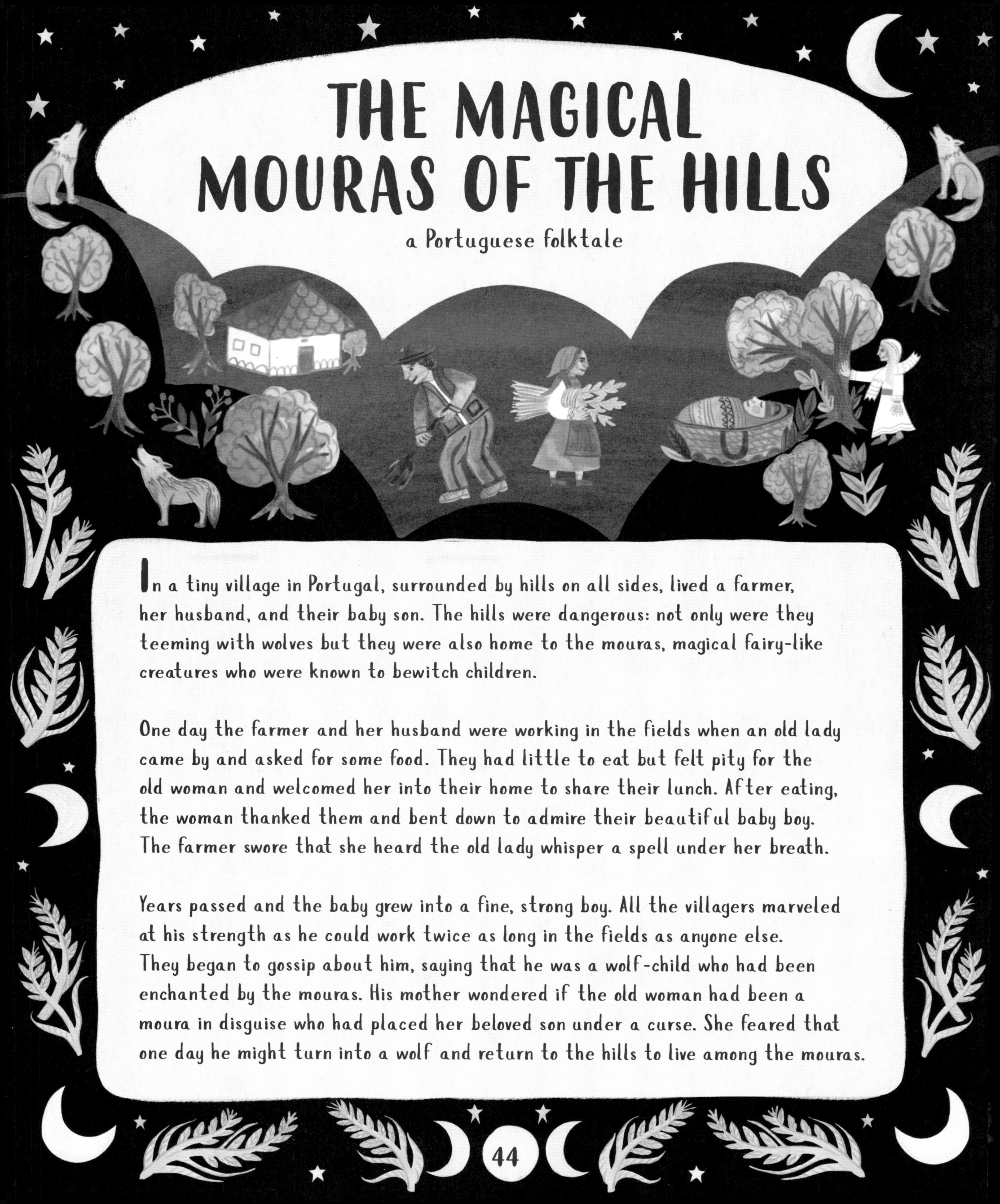

THE MAGICAL MOURAS OF THE HILLS

a Portuguese folktale

In a tiny village in Portugal, surrounded by hills on all sides, lived a farmer, her husband, and their baby son. The hills were dangerous: not only were they teeming with wolves but they were also home to the mouras, magical fairy-like creatures who were known to bewitch children.

One day the farmer and her husband were working in the fields when an old lady came by and asked for some food. They had little to eat but felt pity for the old woman and welcomed her into their home to share their lunch. After eating, the woman thanked them and bent down to admire their beautiful baby boy. The farmer swore that she heard the old lady whisper a spell under her breath.

Years passed and the baby grew into a fine, strong boy. All the villagers marveled at his strength as he could work twice as long in the fields as anyone else. They began to gossip about him, saying that he was a wolf-child who had been enchanted by the mouras. His mother wondered if the old woman had been a moura in disguise who had placed her beloved son under a curse. She feared that one day he might turn into a wolf and return to the hills to live among the mouras.

The next day she noticed the telltale sign of enchantment under her son's arm: the mark of a crescent moon. Full of fear, she went to the village wise-woman and begged her to break the spell. But when she went to fetch her son he was nowhere to be seen.

Months passed and winter drew in. Food was scarce and wolves began to come down from the hills to search for scraps. The villagers took out their guns to defend their food stores. Terrified that someone would capture her son in wolf form and harm him, the farmer set her own trap in the hope of catching him first.

Sure enough, the next morning she discovered an enormous wolf caught in her trap ... and on his leg was the crescent moon symbol! She ran for the wise-woman, who brought her bag of herbs and began to chant a spell. The enchantment lifted before their eyes. There, with his leg still caught in the trap, lay her son. The farmer held him tight and cried tears of joy as she saw that the crescent moon had faded from his arm.

The family lived a long and happy life together in the valley, although the boy was no longer so strong and they never ventured into the hills. Sometimes, when the wind blew, they heard the whispered spells of the mouras floating down from the hills, and they gave thanks that their family was now free from magical mischief.

CREATION STORIES OF HILLS AND VALLEYS

The soft rise and fall of valleys and hills can bring a welcome texture to the landscape. Myths and legends from around the world explain their creation in a variety of intriguing ways.

Some Buddhists believe that the teacher Padmasambhava blessed seven beyul (hidden valleys) in the Himalayas.

In Roman mythology, the Palatine Hill in Rome is where the hero Hercules defeated the fire-breathing giant, Cacus. Hercules struck Cacus with his club so hard that it left a visible dent in the hill.

The Irish gods Tuatha Dé Danann placed the Lia Fáil ("Stone of Destiny") on top of the Hill of Tara.

It was said that the Lia Fáil would roar three times when the rightful High King of Ireland was crowned.

An Indigenous American Ho-Chunk creation story tells that when Earth was first created, it was so smooth that people kept slipping over. When the people begged the Earthmaker for help, he cried a single tear that hit the Earth with such force that it created huge valleys and hills. From that day on, the Earth was uneven and people could walk about without falling.

Spirits in the shape of snowstorms and snow leopards protect the beyul from the outside world. In these wondrous, evergreen places, no one ever grows old.

Dragon Hill in Uffington, England is a small mound where, legend says, Saint George slew a dragon that had been terrorizing local people. Where the dragon's blood spilled on top of the hill, no grass grows, revealing the white chalk underneath.

Beira, goddess of winter, is said to have formed the hills of Scotland using her enormous hammer. Each hill is a different shape so that Beira can recognize where she has been and use them as stepping stones to cross the country.

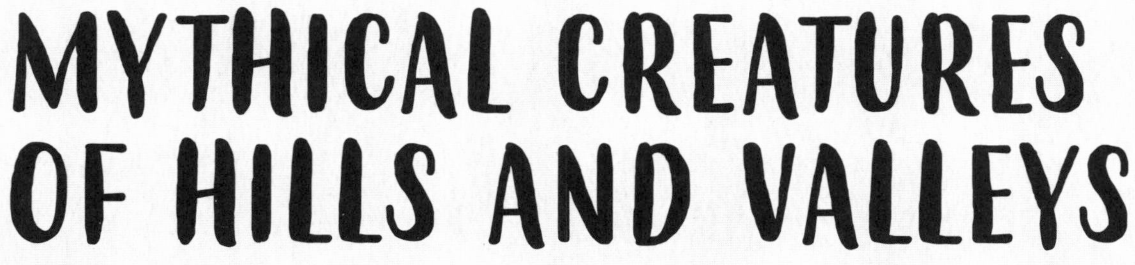

MYTHICAL CREATURES OF HILLS AND VALLEYS

Fairies and trolls are often said to live underneath hills, the landscape acting as a doorway to the fairy realm. The mysterious echoes heard in valleys have also inspired belief in spirits—some kind, others sinister.

In Greek mythology, the Napaeae were beautiful nymphs who protected the valleys. People left offerings of food to win their favor.

Hiisi are spirits of wooded hills in Finnish tradition, similar to trolls in appearance. They chase unwanted visitors from their secluded homes, but cannot enter any place where humans have tamed the land, like villages or farms.

On Midsummer's Eve, celebrations in honor of Aine, the goddess of love, were held at Aine's Hill in Knockainy, Ireland. One year a group of girls stayed late on the hill and Aine appeared to them. When they looked through her magic ring they saw that the hill was alive with dancing fairies.

In Orkney, trows live in dazzling palaces under the rolling hills. Trows are mischievous little creatures who emerge from the hills at night and sneak into homes to warm themselves by the fire.

Fantine are little creatures who live in Switzerland's Vaud valleys. They are kindly to farmers, bringing good weather and giving bells to cows to prevent them from becoming lost.

In Japanese mythology, yamabiko ("mystical valley echo") are friendly, monkey-like spirits with floppy ears. Though rarely seen, their calls create the echoing sounds heard throughout mountains and valleys.

It is said that beneath Blaník Hill in Bohemia (modern-day Czech Republic), is an army of sleeping knights. When Bohemia is under threat, the hill will burst open and the army will wake up and march out, ready to fight.

STANDING STONES AND MEGALITHS

Hills and valleys are often dotted with ancient standing stones called megaliths, sometimes arranged into mysterious circles. Many stories and legends are told to explain how these enormous stones came to be where they are today.

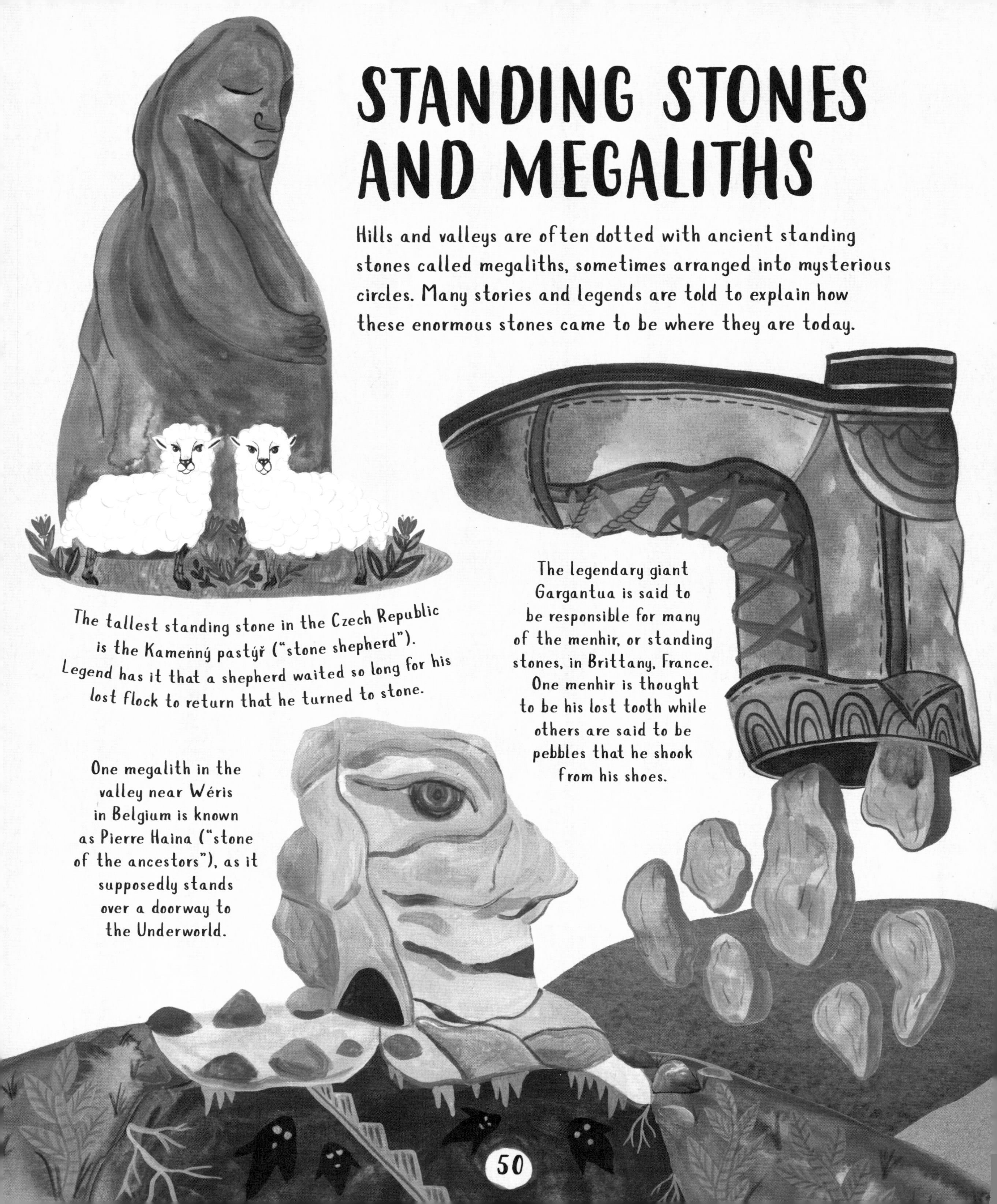

The tallest standing stone in the Czech Republic is the Kamenný pastýř ("stone shepherd"). Legend has it that a shepherd waited so long for his lost flock to return that he turned to stone.

The legendary giant Gargantua is said to be responsible for many of the menhir, or standing stones, in Brittany, France. One menhir is thought to be his lost tooth while others are said to be pebbles that he shook from his shoes.

One megalith in the valley near Wéris in Belgium is known as Pierre Haina ("stone of the ancestors"), as it supposedly stands over a doorway to the Underworld.

When the Greek god Zeus wanted to pinpoint the center of the world, he sent two eagles flying in opposite directions. Where the flights of the eagles crossed, Zeus dropped a stone, known as Omphalos. It landed at Delphi, which was named the center of the world.

The stone circle known as the Ring of Brodgar, in Orkney, is thought to have healing properties. It is said to be the remains of a group of giants who, after dancing all night until dawn, were turned to stone by the rising sun.

The stone circle on Stanton Moor in Derbyshire, England, is known as the Nine Ladies. The story goes that a group of ladies were turned to stone for daring to dance on a Sunday. A tenth stone is said to be the fiddle player who encouraged the dance with his jaunty music.

DRAGONS AND MYTHICAL CAVE-DWELLERS

Deep, dark caves are hidden among hills and valleys around the world. The stories about the dragons, dwarves, and other mysterious creatures who dwell within have fascinated people for centuries.

In Norse mythology, Fafnir was a dwarf who turned into a cave-dwelling dragon to guard the hoard of glittering treasure he stole from his father, until the hero Sigurd slew him. Sigurd then roasted and ate the dragon's heart, which gave him the power to speak to birds.

Kakamora are mischievous, fairy-like creatures from the Solomon Islands who inhabit caves. They are entirely covered in hair and often try to steal fire from humans, because they are unable to make fire themselves.

Welsh folklore tells of two dragons, one white and one red, that slumbered in a cave beneath the hill Dinas Emrys. One day they were awoken and began fighting.

The wizard Merlin foretold that the white dragon (symbolizing England) would win, but that one day the red dragon (symbolizing Wales) would return to defeat its old foe.

Smok was a dragon who dwelt in a cave in Wawel Hill, Poland. He terrorized the townsfolk, eating their animals and attacking their homes. One day, a cunning boy offered Smok a sheep's skin soaked in sulfur, which the dragon quickly devoured. The sulfur made Smok so thirsty that he drank until he exploded!

Alberich is a dwarf king from German tradition. In one tale, he guards the dwarves' underground treasure hoard, wearing a cloak of invisibility that gives him the strength of 12 men. In another, he can only be seen by the wearer of a magic ring, and helps the hero Ortnit in his quests.

WHEN THE RIVERS RAN DRY

an Irish legend

Ireland is known as the Emerald Isle because the many rivers, streams, and springs that criss-cross the country make it a green and fertile land. But long ago, when Ireland was a place of magic, it nearly lost its green hue when the powerful druids who lived there went to war.

The druids were wise and mysterious priests who knew the secret magic of nature. The High King, Cormac mac Airt, kept many druids as advisers. With their help, Cormac hoped to conquer all of Ireland. He marched his army to Munster where he demanded the people pay him high taxes.

When the people of Munster refused to pay, the cruel Cormac commanded his druids to punish them. The druids wove their magic and made all the springs and rivers dry up. Soon the land became cracked and parched, the crops failed, the grass and the trees turned brown, and the people suffered.

King Fiacha of Munster could not stand by and watch his kingdom fall. He begged for the help of Mogh Ruith, one of the most powerful druids in Ireland. Fiacha's men watched in awe as the blind druid flew to them in his ox-driven chariot, lightning flashing from the wheels, making the night sky as bright as day. "Who summons me?" he bellowed as he landed in Fiacha's camp.

"I, Fiacha of Munster, call on you to banish Cormac mac Airt from my lands and bring water back to my people."

The druid smiled and agreed to help, but demanded many rewards: 100 cows, 100 pigs, 100 oxen, 100 fine horses, 50 woven cloaks, and his own piece of land in Munster. It was a steep price, but Fiacha agreed. Mogh Ruith plunged his staff into the ground, creating a huge crack from which torrents of water poured, refilling all the rivers and springs. Then he grew to an enormous height and sucked in a great breath. He breathed out a wild storm that tore through Cormac's camp, turning his warriors to stone. Finally, he summoned the hounds of Hell to chase Cormac and his druids out of Munster for good.

With Cormac defeated, Ireland was at peace. The rivers flowed through the land once more, nourishing the earth and providing food for the people. Though he had asked a heavy price, Mogh Ruith had brought water back to Ireland, making the Emerald Isle green again.

CREATION STORIES OF RIVERS, STREAMS, AND LAKES

Rivers, streams, and lakes provide fresh water to drink and fish to eat. Cultures across the world have long shared stories to explain how these important waterways were formed.

In Greek mythology, Oceanos was a Titan and the source of all fresh water. He and his wife Tethys had more than 6,000 children. They were the Potamoi, who were river gods, and Oceanids, who were nymphs of springs, wells, and fountains.

In Inca mythology, humans once climbed a forbidden mountain to see the sacred fire of the gods. As punishment, the gods sent pumas to eat the humans. This so upset Inti, the Sun god, that he cried for 40 days and 40 nights. His tears created the beautiful Lake Titicaca in the Andes mountains.

According to a tale from Siberia, Russia, a great earthquake once tore a hole in the land. Fire surged upward, threatening to burn down the surrounding villages. In fear, the people prayed to the gods, calling out, "Bay gal!" (which means "fire, stop!" in Buryat). Suddenly cool, fresh water filled the chasm, quenching the flames and forming Lake Baikal.

In legends told by the Patwin people of northern California, before anything else there were Old Badger and Old Frog. Badger was thirsty, so Frog dug a hollow in the ground and filled it with tree sap. Then he created many little frogs who worked together to dig out a lake where they could all drink. This is how California's Clear Lake was formed.

The Ngarrindjeri people of South Australia say that the Murray River was once a tiny stream down which their spiritual ancestor, Ngurunderi, chased Pondi, the giant Murray Cod.

As the enormous fish dashed this way and that, its body carved out the twists and turns of the now-great river.

FOLKLORE OF RIVERSIDE PLANTS

Only certain plants, trees, and flowers can thrive in the wet conditions along river banks. Lotuses and water lilies have been deemed especially magical by many cultures, because they float on the water's surface.

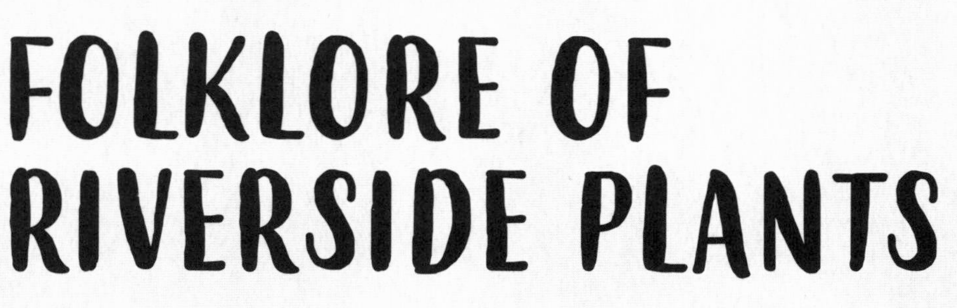

Willow trees often grow next to rivers and so they are strongly linked to water. In English folklore, willow sticks were said to bring good luck to travelers and protect them from bad magic.

Any stretch of water with lots of duckweed growing on its surface could be the hiding place of Jenny Greenteeth, a river spirit from English folklore. She lurked beneath, waiting to pull children and old people into the depths.

In Greek mythology, Iris is a goddess who acts as a messenger for Zeus and Hera. She is represented by a rainbow, linking Heaven and Earth. The flower iris was named in her honor.

The guardian of the Indigenous American Ojibwe people visited a warrior in a dream. She told him that she would protect his people's canoes in the form of a water lily. When the warrior awoke the next day, the whole lake was completely covered in water lilies.

Lotus flowers open in the morning and close at night. In ancient Egypt, the lotus was said to hold the sun, releasing it at dawn and keeping it safe at dusk.

Cardinal flowers are native to North America and are often found by river banks, where hummingbirds flit between them for their nectar. Folklore says that if an elderly woman touches the root of the cardinal flower, she will find true love.

The lotus flower grows from gloopy mud to bloom with bright white flowers. In China, this made it a symbol of purity.

WATER SPRITES AND DEMONS

Many sprites of rivers and lakes are beautiful, like the clear, fresh water they inhabit. But that does not mean that they always have good intentions ...

Rusalki are beautiful Slavic sprites who live in rivers and lakes. They wear robes made of fine water mist and sing enchanting songs. One week, just before summer, rusalki emerge from the rivers and dance through forests in the moonlight. The water droplets that fall from them nourish the earth.

In Arthurian legend, the Lady of the Lake, Nimue, captured the wizard Merlin and buried him under a thorn tree. She wrapped her veil around the tree to make it invisible. But some say that his cry for help is still heard in the rustling of the leaves.

Drac are French demons who dwell in underwater caves, disguised as glittering treasure. As soon as an unwary person tries to claim the riches, the drac transforms into a dragon and pulls them to their doom.

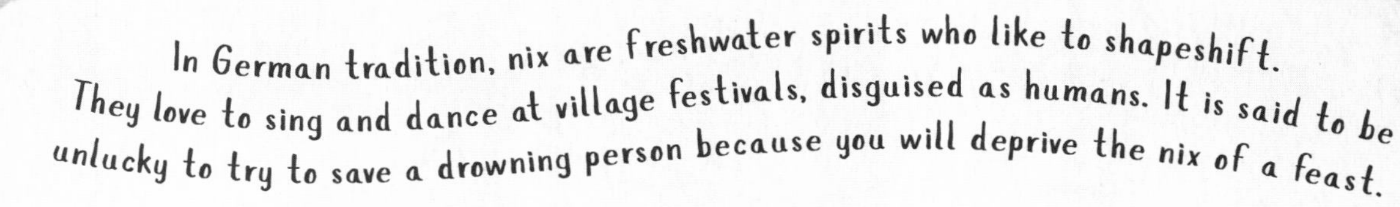

In German tradition, nix are freshwater spirits who like to shapeshift. They love to sing and dance at village festivals, disguised as humans. It is said to be unlucky to try to save a drowning person because you will deprive the nix of a feast.

Kelpie are Scottish water spirits in the form of horses. Any person foolish enough to try to ride one will be pulled into the water and drowned. However, those with the strength to place a bridle on a kelpie can tame it and ride it wherever they like.

From West, Central, and Southern Africa comes the water spirit, Mami Wata. She appears in human form or with the top half of a woman and the bottom half of a fish. Mami Wata carries a huge snake as her constant companion.

MYTHICAL WATER CREATURES

Open water can be dangerous and so stories are told across the world of menacing creatures that lurk in the murky depths. These tales are meant to make children wary of the water and keep them safe.

Cuero inhabits the lakes of Chile, appearing as a cow hide floating on top of the water. With its hooked claws, it grabs unlucky swimmers and pulls them underwater. To defeat it, throw a cactus into the water: the spiky plant will injure the cuero when it tries to take a bite.

Ahuizotl is an Aztec water monster. It looks like a dog, but it has a hand on the end of its long tail which it uses to seize those who wander too close to the water's edge. It is thought to steal the eyes, fingernails, and teeth of its victims.

In Welsh legend, the Afanc is an enormous but invisible water monster. The hero Peredur used a magical stone to make the monster visible so he could defeat it.

Kappa are reptilian water demons from Japan. On their heads are small dips filled with water, which give them the strength to drown their victims. However, their weakness is their manners. If you bow politely when you see one, it will bow in return, causing the water to spill from its head. This forces the kappa to dive underwater to refill it.

You can win a kappa's favor by writing your name on a cucumber (their favorite food) and throwing it into the water.

WATERFALLS, SPRINGS, AND WELLS

Wells and springs have long been valued because of the fresh water they provide to communities. As a result, they are often sacred places.

In Korean mythology, waterfalls were thought to be created whenever dragons, which live in the pools at the bottom of the falls, fly up to heaven.

Gullfloss is a waterfall in Iceland. Its name means "golden waterfall." The story goes that a rich farmer did not want anyone to take his treasure after he died, so he threw his chest of gold into the falls.

In Indigenous American Abenaki legend, trickster raccoon Azban envied the roaring sound of the waterfall, because he thought he was the loudest. Azban stood on the edge of the falls and shouted as loud as he could, but he lost his footing, tumbling into the falls.

The Castalian Spring in Delphi, Greece, was believed to cleanse the souls of all who washed in it. Worshippers bathed there before having their futures told by the Delphic Oracle.

In Irish mythology, Connla's Well was surrounded by nine magical hazelnut trees. When the nuts fell into the water, they produced bubbles of inspiration. The salmon in the well ate nine nuts and gained all the world's knowledge.

Many natural springs in Britain and Ireland are thought to have healing powers. Visitors to wells such as St. Olcan's Well in County Antrim, Ireland, tie a piece of their clothing to a nearby tree. These "rag trees" act as a record of all the sick people cured by the healing waters.

Norse mythology tells that Odin gained great wisdom from Mimir's Well, among the roots of the world tree, Yggdrasil. Mimir let Odin sip from the mystical waters in return for his eye, which Odin threw into the well.

THE LEGEND OF VIXEN TOR

an English folktale

In the middle of Dartmoor, England, stands an ancient rocky mound surrounded by marsh and swamp, known as Vixen Tor. For many years, locals avoided the Tor because in a small cave at its base there lived a wicked old witch.

She was over six feet tall and as thin as a rake. Her eyes were the color of the moss that dotted the rocky moors, and two yellowed teeth hung loosely over her bottom lip. Her hair hung limply about her face like tangles of lichen. Her name was Vixiana, and she hated everything and everyone.

When Vixiana stomped across the moors, sheep scattered from her in fright. Whenever she found a beautiful flower, she snapped it from its stalk. And if she came across a skylark's nest, she made sure to smash each and every egg. But she delighted most in sitting atop the Tor and waiting for a hapless traveler to pass by.

Whenever she spied someone on the path, Vixiana whispered a spell, summoning a thick fog that surrounded the traveler, leaving them confused and lost. She then called out in a kindly voice and guided them through the fog ... straight into her bog. Uttering another spell, she cleared the mist so she could watch gleefully as her victim sank to their death in the swamp. The last sound they heard was her ghastly laugh.

One day, a young man named John was traveling through the moors to visit his family. He lived nearby and knew all about Vixiana and the countless poor souls who had fallen prey to her tricks.

When she spotted John on the path coming toward her, she eagerly set a dense fog swirling about him. But she was dismayed to see him continue walking calmly along the path. For John possessed magical gifts: keen eyes that pierced through any fog, and a ring that could turn him invisible. Through the fog, John saw Vixiana perched upon the Tor, waiting for him to stumble to his doom. Enough was enough. He placed his magic ring on his finger and vanished.

Vixiana leapt up in surprise and scuttled to the edge, craning her neck to see where the traveler had gone. Meanwhile, John climbed the Tor, tiptoed silently up behind her ... and gave her an almighty shove! Vixiana screeched as she tumbled down the side of the mound and landed with a splash in the bog. The thick mud oozed and sucked her into its depths.

The bones of the gruesome witch now lie alongside those of her victims, deep in the swampy ground. Thanks to John, travelers now pass Vixen Tor in safety, knowing that the path ahead will remain clear and that the bog will not claim any more lives.

CREATION STORIES OF WETLANDS

Swamps, marshes, fens, and bogs, where water meets and mingles with land, are often thought to be uniquely magical. Wetlands are also fertile sources of food, fuel, and shelter. They are therefore a common setting for creation stories, and some fascinating folklore is told about the formation of the swamps themselves.

With their dense mists and festering pools of water, the Fens of East Anglia, England, were thought by ancient Britons to be home to dark spirits. Some believed that the strange, damp landscape had formed to keep out Roman invaders.

The Serer people of West Africa believe that the world began as a primordial swamp. From this rich, fertile land grew the very first tree.

In Southern Africa, the Zulu people say that Umvelinqangi, the god with a voice like thunder, created a tiny seed that fell to Earth. The seed became a reed, which multiplied until there was a great swamp covered in reeds. Out of one of the reeds grew the first man, Unkulunkulu.

Ancient Babylonian stories tell that the minor gods, Igigi, were tasked with digging canals in the reed beds, but rebelled against the Anunnaki, their masters. The Anunnaki felt pity for the Igigi and created humans to work the marshes instead.

The Noongar people of Western Australia believe that a giant water snake known as Waugal causes thunder, lightning, and rain. When the world was still forming, Waugal created rivers by winding its body across Earth. Wherever Waugal stopped for a rest, swamps and wetlands took shape.

SPIRITS OF WETLANDS

Shrouded in mist, wetlands often flicker with ghostly lights, caused by natural gases that escape and catch fire on the water. This has given rise to many stories of spirits—some kind, some mischievous, and others wholly evil.

The flames that dot the water in swamps are sometimes known as "jack-o'-lantern" or "will-o'-the-wisp." They were thought to be evil spirits whose glimmer lured travelers into the bottomless bogs.

Some claim that the mysterious lights seen on wetlands are lamps, lit by fairies to assist those who stray from the path and become lost. If you can see the magical lights, it means you have the gift of seeing the future.

In Germany, the "fiery men" are thought to be the spirits of dead people who committed evil in their lifetime. They cannot be welcomed into Heaven, and are doomed to endlessly haunt swamps and marshes.

The bog witch was said to inhabit the swamps that used to cover much of Denmark. She dwelt deep inside the bog, waiting to claim anyone who got sucked into the stinking mire.

The púca is a goblin from Celtic tradition that stalks through marshes holding a lantern. Unwary people followed the light through the treacherous ground until the púca appeared before them, let out a mischievous laugh and blew out the candle, leaving them lost in the pitch-black bog.

The Tiddy Mun was a tiny old man said to live in the Lincolnshire fens, in England. His laugh sounded like the cry of the northern lapwing, or peewit. If a village flooded, its people would go out at night and chant Tiddy Mun's name until they heard his laugh in return. In the morning, the flood waters would have drained away.

MAGICAL CREATURES OF WETLANDS

Swamps, bogs, and marshes are dangerous places, with oozing mud, stagnant pools of filthy water, and thick vegetation. This inhospitable environment has led to some wonderful world folklore about the creatures who might skulk there.

According to Aboriginal Australian lore, bunyips live in swamps called billabongs. They resemble hippos or seals and have a loud, booming cry. They love to eat humans, especially women and children, often hugging them to death.

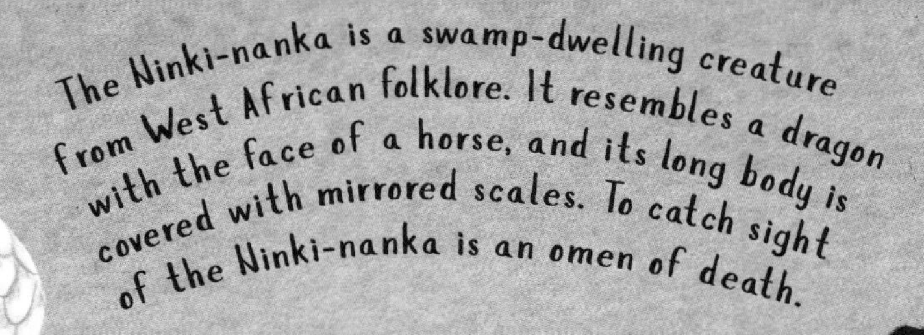

The Ninki-nanka is a swamp-dwelling creature from West African folklore. It resembles a dragon with the face of a horse, and its long body is covered with mirrored scales. To catch sight of the Ninki-nanka is an omen of death.

In Armenian tradition, hotots live deep in the swamps. They emerge from the mire, dripping with sludge and dancing merrily. Any cattle, horses, or children unlucky enough to witness a hotot dancing will fall under its spell, follow it into the marsh and become lost.

American folklore says that the skunk ape lives deep in the Florida swamps. Similar in appearance to Bigfoot, this huge, ape-like creature gives off a terrible smell.
In Greek mythology, the Hydra dwelt in a swamp near Lake Lerna. This serpent had poisonous breath, and if ever it lost one of its nine heads, two more would sprout in its place. When the hero Heracles was tasked with slaying the beast, his nephew Iolaus burned its wounds with a flaming torch, preventing new heads from growing.
Bolotnik is an old man with frog's arms and bug's eyes, and is the master of the marshes in Slavic mythology. Disguising himself as a stepping stone, he tricks people into treading on him before sinking away, causing his victim to fall into the bog.

PLANTS AND FLOWERS OF WETLANDS

In damp, marshy wetlands, only specially adapted plants and flowers can grow. It has often been imagined that these unique species have magical properties.

Meadowsweet is a wetland rose. In Irish tradition, the goddess Aine gave the plant its lovely fragrance, and the hero Cú Chulainn bathed in meadowsweet to calm his rage after battle

Across the British Isles, marsh marigolds have been placed on doorsteps or pushed through letterboxes on May Day eve. The bright yellow flowers were thought to ward off the fairy folk, who get up to mischief on May Day.

The devil's bit scabious has unusally short roots. One story goes that the plant had so many medicinal uses, the devil became jealous and bit off its roots.

In Scottish lore, witches sometimes ride through the sky using a bunch of bulrushes.

The Indigenous American Pueblo nations use bulrushes in traditional rain dances, because the plant grows near water. The Navajo use its leaves as a charm against lightning strikes.

To remember the difference between sedges, rushes, and grasses, use this rhyme from English foklore: "Sedges have edges, rushes are round, and grasses are hollow right up from the ground."

Ragged robin is also known as the cuckoo flower because it blooms when the first cuckoos of spring begin to call. It is linked to Robin Goodfellow, a fairy from English folklore. It was thought unlucky to pick the flower as it would anger the fairies.

GLOSSARY

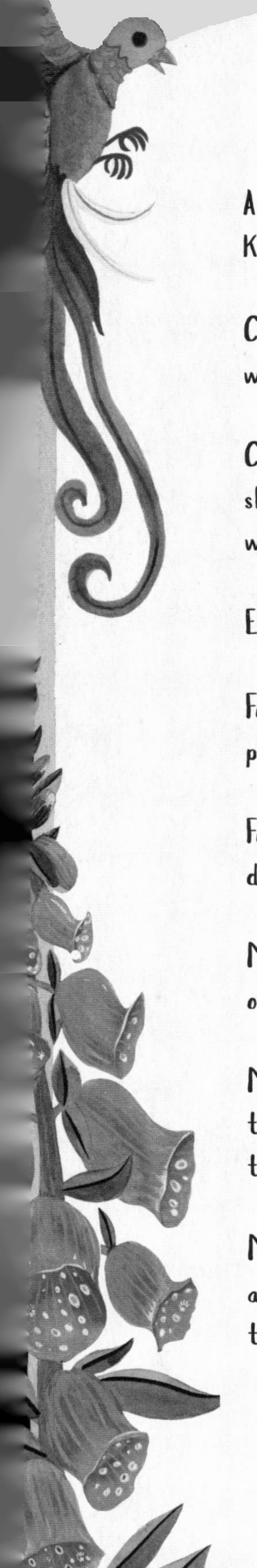

Arthurian – to do with the legendary King Arthur.

Chaos – a state of complete confusion with no order.

Constellation – a group of stars in the sky that form a pattern, often identified with a character from mythology.

Enchanted – placed under a spell.

Folklore – traditional beliefs and customs passed down by word of mouth.

Folktale – traditional stories passed down by word of mouth.

Megalith – a huge stone that is part of a prehistoric monument.

Mirage – an optical illusion caused by the weather, which makes something appear that isn't really there.

Mythology – traditional stories that are used to explain things such as how the world was created.

Organism – any living thing, such as plants, insects, birds, and animals.

Sacred – holy or connected with gods or goddesses.

Sorcerer – a witch or wizard who casts spells.

Sprite – an elf, fairy, or goblin.

Tradition – the passing down of customs, knowledge, and beliefs from generation to generation.

Primeval – to do with the very earliest period in Earth's history.

Primordial – having existed since the very beginning of time.

Underworld – a supernatural world often believed to be underground. In many cultures it is the land of the dead.

INDEX